THE
WONDERS
OF
GRATITUDE

The Blessing of Having a Grateful Heart

Kwaku S. Darkwa, MD

VIKE
SPRINGS
PUBLISHING

THE WONDERS OF GRATITUDE

Published by Vike Springs Publishing Ltd. – London, UK
Contact: admin@vikesprings.com
Website: www.vikesprings.com

First Edition
ISBN-13: 978-1-9998509-4-4 – E-book
ISBN-13: 978-1-9998509-5-1 – Paperback
Printed in the United Kingdom
and the United States of America

To request Dr Darkwa for speaking engagements or interviews, please send an email to: sapondarkwa@yahoo.com

Dr Darkwa's books are available at special discounts when purchased in bulk for promotions or as donations for educational, inspirational and training purposes.

Limit of Liability/Disclaimer of Warranty

"We can complain because rose bushes have thorns, or rejoice because thorns have roses."

Alphonse Karr,
A Tour Round My Garden

"Grateful souls are like fields full of fragrant roses."

Kwaku S. Darkwa

DEDICATION

To Rev. Baafour Ohene Abankwa, thank God our paths crossed. It has been a blessing being your friend.

Contents

CHAPTER ONE
Divine Access

"Give thanks for a little and you will find a lot."
—THE HAUSA OF NIGERIA

GRATITUDE IS SUPPOSED TO BE a 'language' spoken and expressed by people called and cleansed by God. It is what the redeemed should express daily; it is supposed to be seen in their actions and inferred in their speech. It endears the redeemed to their God. It is a truth that God can never really be experienced by the ungrateful. Gratitude is a 'heavenly language', and those who have not learned to appreciate and speak it, cannot be 'accepted' into the manifest presence of God.

Those who belong to the realm where God dwells exude gratitude. This is exactly what the invisible heavenly hosts sing about: gratitude to God and praises to the great King of the universe. They appreciate the ruler of the boundless universe; no wonder they dwell in His very presence. John the Revelator, when he was allowed to see what happens in the heaven of heavens, had this to say about those who dwell in the very presence of God:

Whenever the living creatures give glory, honor and thanks to him who sits on the throne and who lives for ever and ever, the twenty-four elders fall down before him who sits on the throne, and worship him who lives for ever and ever.

They lay their crowns before the throne and say:
"You are worthy, our Lord and God, to receive glory and
honor and power,
for you created all things, and by your will, they were
created and have their being."

—REVELATION 4:9-11

A heart of gratitude lives with a consciousness of God. A state of God-consciousness is a vital requirement to experience the boundless goodness and love of God. Gratitude is a state of the heart that not many mortals have learned to live and walk in, yet it touches the very heart of the Almighty Creator.

It is what makes communicating to the great King easy. The high and exalted One only understands those whose speech is punctuated with thanksgiving. Those who can speak this kind of language well have the great King for their Friend. It is virtually impossible to truly glorify and honour God without a genuine heart full of thanksgiving. We all often dishonour Him by showing our ingratitude when things do not go as we planned. God does not cease to be God when we feel disappointed or let down. We insult the integrity of the great Lord when our attitudes of ingratitude try to portray Jehovah as incapable of changing our situations.

It is a truth that nobody can speak a language well when he or she does not understand it. It becomes noise in the ears of the natives of any land when their language is 'butchered' by strangers. Everyone who does not really understand the language of the natives of any land is a stranger and, therefore, cannot fully enjoy the privileges of that land. Without understanding the language of gratitude, we make ourselves strangers to God. It is a truth that if your tongue is not familiar with words of gratitude, you will not even be permitted into the gates of the 'palace'. Whatever your grievance may be, your case will only be heard if you are permitted to meet with the King. How do you get a hearing with the King when you cannot speak the 'language' that permits you into His palace?

> *Enter his gates with thanksgiving and his courts with praise;*
> *Give thanks to him and praise his name.*
> *For the LORD is good and his love endures forever;*
> *His faithfulness continues through all generations.*
> —PSALM 100:4-5

The 'gatekeepers' have been instructed to permit only those who carry the required permit to enter; without thanksgiving, you remain outside the palace gate. No wonder many people who are ungrateful barely have any peace in their hearts. The God of peace dwells close to those whose hearts are filled with appreciation for even the little things. When the God of peace is absent, inner turmoil rules our hearts.

God is good and loving, so we can trust that He can handle all our issues. He is faithful and can surely be trusted to give us a fair hearing, no matter the case. However, we cannot truly enjoy all these blessings without a heart of gratitude.

God has always been approached with gratitude, and this is the tradition of the kingdom of God. Your prayers will not even be heard when you have an ungrateful heart. Our hearts, hardened by sin, make us 'wicked' by nature. The prayer of such an individual is an abomination to God. It is natural for any father to feel indifferent about a son who has shown over and again gross ingratitude. Why, then, do we assume that God will gladly welcome our pleas when we have acted towards Him in a similar manner?

In his hour of distress and gloom, the psalmist remembered the days when he used to join the procession to the house of God. In the midst of discouragement over the turn of events in his life, David remembered that God is his hope. Most importantly, he remembered he and others gained the audience of the King in the years gone by, approaching Him with thanksgiving:

> *How I used to go with the multitude, leading the procession to the house of God, with shouts of joy and thanksgiving among the festive throng.*
> —PSALM 42:4

True gratitude is what makes the Father always pleased to welcome us into His courts. Which content father ever refuses audience with his cherished children? A heart of gratitude pushes away all the obstacles that stand between our heavenly Father and us. It makes every other issue secondary to the King, as far as our issues are concerned.

Gratitude knows the way around many difficulties. When we make Him our Friend, He will help us, even in our moments of confusion. He directs all those who endear themselves to Him, showing them the route back to the King's palace, no matter how far they may have veered off.

Gratitude opens our hearts to experience God. It will put joy back on our faces and set us back in a festive mood. Gratitude drives away the influence of panic and brings us into the very presence of the merciful God.

Come with a Good Sacrifice

All who come to the 'palace' seeking the favour of the King should come with a gift. Your gift will hasten your access to His courts. This is how you hasten divine protocol. It is very wrong to come to God without anything to offer Him. He deserves a gift because He is the High and exalted One. The subjects of the King are expected to honour Him with gifts and offerings. These gifts do not necessarily have to be material things.

Gratitude is a gift acceptable to God any day if it is genuinely offered from our hearts. We may not have silver or gold, bulls or goats, but hearts full of gratitude are better than all the silver or gold a man can give to God in his or her lifetime. On countless occasions, God reminded the people of Israel that a sacrifice of thanksgiving was worth more than the sacrifice of hundreds of bulls.

> *"Hear, O my people, and I will speak O Israel, and I will testify against you: I am God, your God. I do not rebuke you for your sacrifices or your burnt offerings, which are ever before me. I have no need of a bull from your stall or of goats from your pens, for every animal of the forest is mine, and the cattle on a thousand hills. I know every bird in the mountains, and the Creatures of the field are mine. If I were hungry, I would not tell you, for the world is mine, and all that is in it. Do I eat the flesh of bulls or drink the blood of goats? Sacrifice thanks offerings to God, fulfill your vows to the Most High, and call upon me in the day of trouble; I will deliver you, and you will honor me."*
>
> —PSALM 50:7-15

We should learn to be thankful, even when we find

ourselves in the valleys of life, knowing that He who was gracious to us yesterday can do the same today.

The best time to be thankful for God's mercies and to sing songs of His goodness is when times are difficult; then it becomes a sacrifice. A gift becomes a sacrifice when it really costs us so much, and yet, we release it to God, knowing that He deserves even more than we can offer. It is easy to give God our gratitude when everything around us is okay. However, when the situation we find ourselves in is unpleasant, thanksgiving becomes a task; it then becomes a sacrifice.

> *Let them sacrifice thank offerings and tell of his works with songs of joy.*
> —Psalm 107:22

Grateful Souls

There are people who have not gone to school, may not live in nice homes, eat good food or speak good grammar, yet they live as if they have no problems. That, I believe, is what is peculiar with many Africans. They are poor but happy. They are glad and thankful for the many small blessings they receive daily. Many have to fend for themselves at quite an early age, and despite all the challenges they face daily, they look forward to tomorrow with great hope. Amazingly, these are the ones who believe in God and trust God to open bigger doors and opportunities to them tomorrow. I believe, by having such optimistic hearts and thankful souls, they are, themselves, an example of those who live offering sacrificial thanks to God.

These ones are focused on what they have and are not too bothered about what they do not have. With such an attitude, they can see opportunities that lay ahead and **do not focus** on the regrets of what was missed yesterday. These ones lean on one another and have more meaningful relationships. They are more social in their outlook and have learnt that life is more than thinking about what they have or do not have. To many Africans, even funerals are turned into social gatherings, and this helps infuse some joy and happiness into the sadness of death and loss. In spite of all the challenges these souls face, their hearts have learnt to offer a sacrifice of thanksgiving.

CHAPTER TWO
True Gratitude

"If the only prayer you say in your life is thank you, that would suffice."
—MEISTER ECKHART

Gratefulness Dispels Gloom

TRUE GRATITUDE IS LIKE A life spring: it erupts from deep down the heart and not from the mind. True gratitude is not just in what we say and do, but it is what our hearts communicate, no matter how subtle that is. It can never really be silenced or subdued; it is a forceful spring that affects everything you do. It is actually what makes the heart sing. It affects everything about a person: his or her speech, demeanour and actions.

True gratitude is also a manifestation of grace bestowed on men who appreciate little mercies. It is a grace that calms the spirit, allays our fears and assures us that it will be well. It brightens the eyes to see the blessing of today and the brightness and hope of a better tomorrow. It dispels gloom and brings sunlight and warmth into our hearts. True gratitude cannot be feigned or copied.

Spoken gratitude is not necessarily heartfelt; it could just be hypocritical. This is also why it is very unwise to trust a man just because of what he or she says. Men will try to sing your praises and say all kinds of good things about you in your presence, yet they will curse you the moment you turn your back. Jesus did not entrust himself to any man; He knows what is in man (John 2:23-25).

It is a truth that God weighs the hearts of men and not just the gravity of their words. He looks into our hearts to ascertain whether we truly mean what we say and do. About Israel, God says:

> *"These people honor me with their lips, but their hearts are far from me."*
>
> —MATTHEW 15:8

Men honour other men with their lips, but their hearts are far from them. Do not make the mistake of reading the 'lips' of men. It is almost always not what they really mean.

The School of Gratitude and Honour

Life has a school where gratitude and honour for those who have helped us are woven into the very fibres of our 'hearts'. These schools are not sited among the affluent and the very privileged, but they are abundant among the underprivileged and deprived.

Their lessons on gratitude and honour are taught daily to the poor and unrespected. These ones have known one form of sorrow or the other, and they now appreciate what it means to be privileged in even the smallest possible way. They do not take anything for granted, no matter how small. They have learnt to take life one day at a time and be grateful for God's tender mercies. They appreciate life and its little blessings, and they have learnt to be thankful for everything, even in the midst of uncertainty and apparent gloom.

Grateful souls are thankful for life itself. They see it as a privilege to rise every morning and to see the sunset every evening. They know that they owe their very existence to the Almighty. They are thankful for health in the midst of endemic diseases and sound mind in the midst of many who are depressed and frustrated. Even when they do not know where tomorrow's meal will come from, they eat the little they have today with much gladness.

They consider the little they have today as plenty and with much gratitude. They understand what it means to serve the Lord in their present estate, and they know the consequences of being ungrateful. They have learnt from history what happened to Israel after they became ungrateful in the midst of all God had graciously provided for them.

They remember what has been decreed for the wicked and the ungrateful:

> *Because you did not serve the LORD your God joyfully and gladly in the time of prosperity, therefore in hunger and thirst, in nakedness and dire poverty, you will serve the enemies the LORD sends against you. He will put an iron yoke on your neck until he has destroyed you.*
> —Deut 28:46-48–NIV

They have graduated from the elementary school of pride and self-reliance to the class of those who lean on the dependable God. They have known one form of need or another (not necessarily financial), for none can be truly grateful unless they have met with and been taught by 'the professor' called need.

To be truly grateful is to learn how to be content with little or with plenty. When we are grateful in the season of lack, God will lift us up into plenty. A lot of people who are arrogant and snobbish have not really been tutored by the seasons of lack. They believe they are entitled to the best of everything and have no regard for the Lord whose mercies sustain all men.

It is a truth that many who have been lifted to the place of prominence and still maintain their humility have crossed the path of dire need before. Disadvantage and lack have a way of working humility into the hearts of the living. The apostle Paul was taught gratitude and humility through what he went through. He came to a place in his life's journey when he confessed that life situations had taught him an invaluable lesson:

> *I know what it is to be in need, and I know what it is to have plenty. I have learned the secret of being content in any and every situation, whether well fed or hungry, whether living in plenty or in want.*
> —Philippians 4:12 -NIV

True gratitude is learning to be content with the little you have been blessed with. It is important to realize that the little you have is still a blessing. It all depends on what lenses you look at them through. The earlier you learn this, the better life will treat you. True appreciation for little mercies opens doors of progress to us.

Gratitude and humility make their abode in the 'valleys' of life, and most often you will only get to know them when life's situations send you to their dwellings. The valleys of life may not be nice places to dwell in, but they do teach us priceless lessons in this life. They prepare us to handle adversity positively. They teach us how to cope with similar situations we will have to pass through on our way to our places of blessing and abundance. They build the confidence in us that we can handle whatever life throws at us (Philippians 4:13). They place into our hands an invisible certificate that qualifies us to occupy and influence places of our uplifting.

Many who find themselves in positions of blessing and prominence without possessing a certificate from the school of gratitude will be sent back to acquire one in the valley.

Reduced by Pride

"Many people who order their lives rightly in all other ways are kept in poverty by their lack of gratitude."
—WALLACE WATTLES

Many have lost their positions of elevation in life because they have regard for neither man nor God. They have failed time and again to genuinely say thank you to the Lord God and to their fellow men who have helped them in one way or another. They fail to appreciate the truth that a heart of gratitude endears them to God and man. They live in the arrogance and fullness of themselves and directly or indirectly 'insult' God and those He made in His image. They behave and speak as if they are gods and often forget that this earth is the abode of men like them: mere mortals.

Man must always remember that he is just a string of bones joined by cartilage and clothed with 'conditioned and polished mud'. We have all been programmed to deteriorate and decay at a set time.

Teach us to number our days aright, that we may gain a heart of wisdom.
—PSALM 90:12-NIV

The reality of our inescapable appointment with death should help us all to walk in humility. When we fail to appreciate this reality, then even the beasts of the field become of more value than us. When we lose sight of the fact that death awaits all of us, we walk in pride and baneful arrogance.

When gratitude is absent from our hearts, a haughty spirit tries to take over. We then see all things through our prideful eyes and, obviously, assume they have little value. Men who possess hearts of ingratitude often have haughty spirits and, consequently, haughty eyes. The scriptures categorically tell us how God sees all who have haughty eyes: He abhors them. He sets Himself against such people, virtually 'fighting' them Himself.

There are six things the LORD hates, seven that are detestable to him: haughty eyes...
—PROVERBS 6:16-17-NIV

God lifts up the humble, but He opposes the proud. Pride eventually demotes; it drowns all who hang onto it. The Biblical example of King Nebuchadnezzar is a vivid story of how God sets Himself against the proud. It is a humbling story of how a great and mighty king was reduced to 'nothing' in order to teach him to be thankful and appreciate the God of heaven, who rules over the affairs of men (Daniel 4:30-37).

From Grace to Grass

"What separates privilege from entitlement is gratitude."
—Brené Brown

No matter how high we climb in life, we should learn to appreciate the fact that even when we believe we deserve our places in life, it is still God who enables us all. He is sovereign over all, and all exist and have their being because He allows them to. No one from the east or the west or from the desert can exalt a man. But it is God who judges: He brings one down, He exalts another (Psalm 75:6-7).

The very breath of life in our nostrils is not ours to control. In fact, we are too frail as fleshly beings to boast about anything we accomplish. This should make us humble rather than proud. As we look to the benevolence of heaven to sustain us daily, we humbly ask for God's protection and covering so we may continue to do what we do so well.

A story is told about a very rich man who had everything going for him. He was so successful that he took it for granted that things would always continue as such. Success breeds some subtle form of pride within all of us. It makes us too inward looking and a bit too 'self-reliant'. This rich man's grounds produced him a good crop as usual. He had so much produce that he was overwhelmed. Instead of being grateful for the great harvest, his whole attention was to himself, his prowess and his harvest. Success had made him blind to the truth that we owe God so much, the least being the very breath of our lives.

Everything does not have to rotate around us and our daily breakthroughs. There is more to life than what we have achieved or the providential positions we have attained.

*And he (Jesus) told them this parable: "The ground of
a certain rich man produced a good crop. He thought
to himself, 'What shall I do? I have no place to store
my crops.' "Then he said, 'This is what I'll do. I will tear
down my barns and build bigger ones, and there I will
store all my grain and my goods. And I'll say to myself,
"You have plenty of good things laid up for many years.
Take life easy; eat, drink and be merry."' "But God said to
him, 'You fool! This very night your life will be demanded
from you. Then who will get what you have prepared for
yourself?'"*

—LUKE 12:16-20

When we fail to give honour to those to whom honour
is due, we set ourselves against the Great Provider. When
all that is in our thoughts are *me, myself and I,* we behave
foolishly, and foolish people do not deserve to live and
enjoy what they believe they have laboured for. What you
do not surrender to God, you will eventually lose. It is
wisdom to hand over to Him what you cannot keep.

Whatever God enables you to acquire, it is He alone
who enables you to keep. To live your life as if it is all
about what you can make of it and what you can keep is
gross ingratitude and gross disrespect to Him. This is the
undoing of many who believe everything they ever have is
their doing. A heart of gratitude does not focus entirely on
its strength; it focuses on God's strength and ability.

A heart of gratitude does not take any blessing in life for
granted; it sees every blessing as a privilege. It does not
speak presumptively; it acknowledges its frailty and obvious
limitations. It takes a humble heart to continue to 'reign' in
this life. It takes humility for God to lift you up and even
more humility to stay in the place of your uplifting.

Humility helps us to encounter grace that lifts us up and still maintains the grace upon our lives. Where humility is absent, grace ceases to operate. Destruction and decay then lay their grip upon us, and then 'grass' bids us welcome. If we will not humble ourselves, God will not bother Himself with us, allowing misfortune to humble us.

CHAPTER THREE
Living Simply

"Simplicity is the ultimate sophistication."
—Leonardo Da Vinci

Time to Prioritise

As we are finding better ways of making life more comfortable, we are chasing after money. This chase has also entangled our lives with a lot of activity. The more activity we engage in, the more confusion we embrace. Confusion will upset your soul, and your spirit will be pushed down and under. A depressed soul cannot walk in gratitude. You will do well to rid your life of all the unnecessary activity that contributes to all the confusion you may be dealing with.

There are so many things in life we are supposed to be grateful for. All the activities that keep us so busy may be hindering our view from seeing the many simple things in life we should be grateful for. Very often we are doing so many things and have not sat down to prioritise what is essential and what is not. Indeed, it amounts to "much ado about nothing"! Many times, our souls are cluttered by too many activities. We are stressed at the workplace and in the home too.

Worry about the basic necessities of life may put you on edge and render you unappreciative of the blessings of God around you. Anxiety in life may spring from not knowing where your next meal is coming from. God created us to live simply, but we all find ourselves engulfed and battling all kinds of things in this complex world. You may be worried about what you will put on or where you will lay your head. Your fear of how things will turn out for your family may be a great concern to you. You are justified as any rational human being to bother about all the uncertainties of life. You need to take one day at a time and allow God to do what He will do in your life as you play your own role well.

Take responsibility for your tomorrow, and plan and work towards it. However, do not allow what is out of place to mess up your today. All the running around you are doing may contribute to making your life more complex and difficult. You may not need all the clutter and activity in your life. Sit back and assess your life and all the activities that keep you harassed. Look at what is necessary and what is not. Some things are important but may not be necessary right now in your life's journey. Deal with what is necessary today, and prioritise on what is needed now. Although many things may be important, the timing may not be right presently.

If your life is so complex that you barely notice and appreciate the presence of birds flying around you, it means you are too busy and too worried. You need to be less encumbered by your day-to-day problems to be able to notice the provision of a mighty hand taking care of this boundless universe. The earth alone and all of the life that fills it, including your life, is an amazing work of a supernatural hand in an extraordinarily planned creation. There is a God who provides, and we need to be free at heart and in our minds to appreciate this truth.

If your heart cannot be mesmerised by the beauty and fragrance of the flowers of the fields, then you are too worried or too busy. When you are simple at heart and unburdened by life's problems, you will not only notice the beauty around you, but you will also appreciate the day-to-day changes occurring, even among the common grass on the lawn and in the lilies of the field. There is a silent glory ministering to us all of the time, but when our lives are too burdened by the challenges around us, we will equally fail to appreciate all the wonders and blessings around us.

> *"Therefore, I tell you, do not be anxious about your life, what you will eat or what you will drink, nor about your body, what you will put on. Is not life more than food, and the body more than clothing? Look at the birds of the air: they neither sow nor reap nor gather into barns, and yet your heavenly Father feeds them. Are you not of more value than they? And which of you by being anxious can add a single hour to his span of life? And why are you anxious about clothing? Consider the lilies of the field, how they grow: they neither toil nor spin, yet I tell you, even Solomon in all his glory was not arrayed like one of these. But if God so clothes the grass of the field, which today is alive and tomorrow is thrown into the oven, will he not much more clothe you, O you of little faith?"*
> —MATTHEW 6:25-34

Different Race Tracks

Never compare your life to that of another. In our quest to achieve success, we end up comparing ourselves to others. We start comparing what we have with what others have acquired, and we are very dissatisfied with our lot. We want what others have, and we begin chasing for more and more. We are indirectly running a race by chasing for more and more that we presume will give us a significant advantage over others. Competition is great, especially healthy competition, but we need to keep something in view: we are not all running the same race, and we are all on different tracks in life.

Do not embrace a mediocre life, but also, do not put yourself in an unhealthy quest to be like everybody else. All fingers are not equal: some are longer than others. Many of the things we yearn for, apart from the basic necessities of life, may bring many sorrows and unforeseen problems along with them.

> *But godliness with contentment is great gain, for we brought nothing into the world, and we cannot take anything out of the world. But if we have food and clothing, with these we will be content. But those who desire to be rich fall into many senseless and harmful desires that plunge people into ruin and destruction.*
> —1Timothy 5:6-9

Watch Your Cravings

We need to watch our cravings carefully so that they do not push us into trouble. May your desire not be driven by what others have or have acquired. Wrong cravings will lead you onto wrong paths. Many have wandered from the path of safety and gratitude because of all kinds of desires motivated by evil. Many times, watching other people and what they have blind us to pursue the 'prosperity' we already have.

"Whatever our individual troubles and challenges may be, it's important to pause every now and then to appreciate all that we have, on every level. We need to literally 'count our blessings', give thanks for them, allow ourselves to enjoy them, and relish the experience of prosperity we already have."
—Shakti Gawain

We Are Custodians on Earth

Everything that we are blessed to have has been put into our custody. We are just custodians here on earth. The more we have, the more we have to give account for. To whom much is given, more will be required. Do not be envious of all that is happening in the life of others. Just ask God to give you what you need, and that should be okay. If you ask for more, ask for more to be a blessing to others. The more you are given, the more likely that you may mismanage what has been given to you and even get to the point where you forget God, your true and lasting source. The words of wisdom from Agur in the book of Proverbs sheds more light on this:

Remove far from me falsehood and lying; give me neither poverty nor riches; feed me with food that is needful for me, lest I be full and deny you and say, "Who is the LORD?" or lest I be poor and steal and profane the name of my God.
—Proverbs 30: 8-9

Prosperity beyond what wisdom and strength we have to manage can pull us down. We need to pray that we will always treasure the words of God more than any portion of food or substance that satisfies our wants. We should learn to be satisfied with what we have for the day. Our portions for the day should gladden our hearts, and we should also be grateful that we have seen today and have been provided for to see us through the day. We should spend our efforts on dealing with today's challenges and not be burdened by all that the uncertain tomorrow brings with it. This is the wisdom in asking for our daily bread. Sufficient for today is today's trouble. When we have the right perspective, we will have the strength to see us through our daily challenges. We need to be grateful for today, and this could be all we say in our prayer to our Maker. As Jesus said, "tomorrow will take care of itself".

"If the only prayer you say in your life is thank you, that would suffice."
—MEISTER ECKHART

CHAPTER FOUR
The Invisible Shields

"Gratitude is a mark of a noble soul and a refined character. We like to be around those who are grateful."
—JOSEPH B. WIRTHLIN

Your Heart Condition

IT IS A TRUTH THAT we attract or repel things around us by the energies our hearts emit. There are certain characteristics that some positive souls possess and exhibit which draw people to them. Similarly, there are also some negative characteristics and traits that push people away from some individuals. Just as vultures draw close to a carcass, so does a flower attract bees. Something within you will either draw good to you or repel good from you. The condition of your heart will either attract good or evil towards you. We can attract help or trouble by the predisposition of our hearts.

> *The LORD is my strength and my shield; in him my heart trusts, and I am helped; my heart exults, and with my song, I give thanks to him.*
> —PSALM 28:7

Have you ever paused to assess why you are drawing the kind of attention to yourself that you are? Do you understand why some good things are not coming towards you? Why do you think the wrong crowd is excited about approaching you?

There is this story about a young girl who had come of age and was thinking about getting married and settling down. She was beautiful, quite well-educated and was pleasant to be with. Her parents had always dreamed that a young and wealthy man would come and ask for her hand in marriage. This was, however, not happening, and they got worried. They noticed that a 'different' class of young men, who were not ready to settle down, and middle-aged married men were those who flocked around their daughter, and obviously, they were very worried.

What was attracting this calibre of men towards this young lady? Why was she not attracting the type of men that every parent would be glad to have as a son-in-law? Her dressing was almost always too skimpy and 'sexy'. She gave a wrong signal to the men around her. She was emitting the wrong type of energy. She was 'easy and available', and this attracted the wrong type of 'bees'. The 'naughty' young men were attracted to her poorly clad figure, and the married men also wanted to use her because that was the message she was indirectly sending across.

What you serve will draw you a calibre of 'customer'. There are invisible shields that are in place when a young woman dresses with dignity and respects herself. This shield will ward off many unsuitable suitors. When we compromise on what is decent and respectable, we will draw disrespect to ourselves, and in doing so, a very wrong type of people.

The Need to Develop a Heart of Gratitude

A similar situation occurs within our inner person. We are always emitting some form of energy: good or bad. Hence, we are consequently attracting good or bad energies. God's presence is drawn to a certain nature of heart and attitude. Gratitude dispositions cause our hearts to attract the attention and presence of God. Ingratitude, likewise, creates an inner environment that repels God's Spirit and all the blessings that come with Him. In essence, when we have God on our side, there are many blessings that flow into our lives. When He is not happy with us because of sin, we stand to lose a lot. This is one major reason why the enemy will want you to disobey God and His word. When we do so, we open ourselves up for the enemy to enter into certain arenas of our lives and wreak havoc.

A heart of gratitude endears us to our Maker. It keeps His presence close to us and around us. This is another reason why complaining all the time about our troubles and problems is not good. Not only does it 'disempower' God in our lives, but it also keeps Him away from us. Nobody likes to live with and be company to a nagging and ungrateful soul. Why do we suppose that God would like to stay around us when we exhibit such a nature? When we live and walk in ingratitude, we grieve God's Spirit, and when He is grieved, He keeps a distance from us. This lifts up certain walls of protection from us and exposes us to the wrath of darkness.

> *For since the creation of the world God's invisible qualities—his eternal power and divine nature—have been clearly seen, being understood from what has been made, so that people are without excuse. **For although they knew God, they neither glorified him as God nor gave thanks to him**, but their thinking became futile and their foolish hearts were darkened. Although they claimed to be wise, they became fools and exchanged the glory of the immortal God for images made to look like a mortal human being and birds and animals and*

reptiles.

Therefore God gave them *over in the sinful desires of their hearts to sexual impurity for the degrading of their bodies with one another. They exchanged the truth about God for a lie, and worshiped and served created things rather than the Creator—who is forever praised. Amen. Because of this,* ***God gave them over*** *to shameful lusts. Even their women exchanged natural sexual relations for unnatural ones. In the same way the men also abandoned natural relations with women and were inflamed with lust for one another. Men committed shameful acts with other men, and received in themselves the due penalty for their error.*

Furthermore, just as they did not think it worthwhile to retain the knowledge of God, so ***God gave them over*** *to a depraved mind, so that they do what ought not to be done. They have become filled with every kind of wickedness, evil, greed and depravity. They are full of envy, murder, strife, deceit and malice. They are gossips, slanderers, God-haters, insolent, arrogant and boastful; they invent ways of doing evil; they disobey their parents; they have no understanding, no fidelity, no love, no mercy. Although they know God's righteous decree that those who do such things deserve death, they not only continue to do these very things but also approve of those who practice them.* (Emphasis mine).

—ROMANS 1: 20-32

The above text from the book of Romans clearly shows that failure to glorify God's greatness and appreciate His provision or show gratitude exposes us to negative elements that always seek to have control over us. The darkness around us is kept at bay from our hearts and minds by our sense of gratitude and choosing to glorify the Creator instead of His creation. When we fail to thank God for His goodness yet go our way to do what we deem right or contrary to what He has planned for us, darkness will engulf our hearts and souls.

There are invisible shields all around the grateful and thankful soul that keep darkness at a distance. There is a force of protection around the person who has given God His rightful place in his life and continually shows appreciation to the Maker of all men. When God's presence leaves us, evil takes over. There was a king in Israel so many years ago called King Saul. He was taken from among his father's sons and made king beyond his wildest dreams to rule over the nation of Israel and to govern God's people. When he forgot where God had picked him from and showed ingratitude and disobedience to God's word, he lost the presence of God and immediately an evil spirit possessed his soul.

> *Enter his gates with thanksgiving and his courts with praise; give thanks to him and praise his name. For the Lord is good and his love endures forever; his faithfulness continues through all generations.*
>
> —PSALM 100:4-5

Thanksgiving brings us into the presence of God. It keeps us close to God and His Spirit and opens us up to His goodness. It is not a mistake that we enter into God's gates (His very presence and courts) when we have a heart of thanksgiving and praise. There are surely invisible shields within, through which we enjoy protection by God's abiding presence and love, when we live and walk in thanksgiving to God for His benevolence towards us. Outside of His gates, there is trouble lurking all around. We move out into enemy territory and reach anytime we are outside God's gates and courts. We slowly slip into enemy terrain when we show ingratitude for God's goodness and fail to glorify Him.

Do Not Underestimate His Benefits

There is a tendency to underestimate the blessings of God. Not all His blessings can be seen and quantified. Even the side benefits of living in thanksgiving to God cannot be quantified. Job, a man who lived many years ago, knew and understood this. This explains why he would still give glory to God, even when things were not going well with him. He knew there were immense direct and indirect blessings to serving God, being thankful and glorifying God for every little mercy that comes our way.

> *"Naked I came from my mother's womb, and naked I will depart. The Lord gave and the Lord has taken away; may the name of the Lord be praised."*
> —JOB 1:21 NIV

Even the enemy, Satan, is aware of the numerous blessings of walking with God. We need to be grateful for everything that goes well for us and with us no matter how small.

> *"Does Job fear God for nothing?" Satan replied.*
> *"Have you not put a hedge around him and his household and everything he has? You have blessed the work of his hands, so that his flocks and herds are spread throughout the land."*
> —JOB 1:9-10

There surely are invisible hedges or shields around us that the normal eye cannot see. These are very effective at keeping unseen forces at bay. We will do well to remember that one sure way of keeping these shields intact is by living with hearts that glorify God continually and showing gratitude for every small mercy.

CHAPTER FIVE
Conditioned for the Mysterious

"The moment one gives close attention to anything, even a blade of grass, it becomes a mysterious, awesome, indescribably magnificent world in itself."
—Henry Miller

A Heart of Appreciation Is an Open Door

GRATITUDE OPENS OUR EYES WIDER to see an entire world of magnificence that is hidden from ungrateful souls. It leads to the doors that open us to the reality of how privileged we truly are. It makes our vision better and our focus sharper. It helps us to appreciate the little we have today as we wait for what we do not have but perceive from afar. We will see progress in our lives, even with little changes, no matter how small. It will further direct us to say thank you for even simple things. We will see the little we have as plenty, and this will set the stage for God to do what He does best: make things happen for us. God is still in the business of making things happen for grateful souls. When He is pleased, He cannot sit still; He is moved to do more and more of what He intends to do.

Sing to the LORD with thanksgiving; make music to our God on the harp.
He covers the sky with clouds; he supplies the earth with rain and makes grass grow on the hills.
He provides food for the cattle and for the young ravens when they call.
His pleasure is not in the strength of the horse, nor his

delight in the legs of a man;
the LORD delights in those who fear him, who put their
hope in his unfailing love.

—PSALM 147:7-11-NIV

God is not excited just because what He created is awesome. He is not excited by the graceful strides of a horse in motion, nor does its strength amuse Him. He does not get fascinated when men use whatever He endows them with. He delights in the true gratitude and praises of His creation.

Nobody can truly show gratitude to God without appreciating His awesomeness; this is genuine 'fear' of the Lord. When we are truly appreciative, we indirectly show our hope in Him. True appreciation triggers excitement in God. When God is excited, miracles follow inevitably. He will then create even what has not been before. His miracle-working power flows through gratitude. God 'cannot' be stopped when something excites Him.

A heart of gratitude stirs up the supernatural. This is the same kind of excitement God had when creation began. Everything He made gave Him the 'kick' for the next creation: Genesis 1:21. Creation sang the gratitude and praises of its Creator as it is documented in the Biblical book of Job:

"Where were you when I laid the earth's foundation?
Tell me, if you understand.
Who marked off its dimensions? Surely you know!
Who stretched a measuring line across it?
On what were its footings set, or who laid its cornerstone-
while the morning stars sang together and all the angels
shouted for joy?"

—JOB 38:4-7

And God saw that what He made was good. The creation appreciated and had great hope in its Creator; no wonder God kept creating and creating. When God is excited about you, you can go and 'rest' knowing He will do something about your situation.

The Excited Mediator

The term mediator is used here for one who steps into a situation to make things happen. He is the vital and essential link who makes it all possible. God is the Mediator who enables the supernatural to occur among men. He steps into a situation only when our hearts are conditioned to please Him.

There is nothing that catches God's attention more than a heart of gratitude. This is the heart of a man whose heart is united in gratitude and loyal dependence upon God for His mediation in the affairs of his life.

> *For the eyes of the LORD run to and fro throughout the whole earth,*
> *to show Himself strong on behalf of those whose heart is loyal to Him.*
> —2 CHRONICLES 16:9 NKJV

God shows He is strong on behalf of those whose hearts are loyal to Him. An individual with a heart that exudes dependence upon God and appreciation is the kind of heart that automatically invites God to step into any situation, no matter how difficult. When we say we know God, our hearts are supposed to show loyalty to God if we expect Him to be loyal to us. God is actually eager to move into action on our behalf. In fact, His eyes run to and fro looking for a man who has positioned himself for a breakthrough.

Jesus Christ Our Great Example

One of the reasons why Jesus' ministry was a success was because He lived with a conscious awareness of His dependent union with the heavenly Father, and His heart was always full of gratitude for it. Not surprising that God always stepped in any time He needed an intervention. Jesus carried a heart full of gratitude. Not only did He put off His divine nature, but He took on the nature of mere men. As a mortal, He now became totally dependent on God, gratefully trusting that He could fully rely on the Almighty. The 'man' Christ Jesus knew that it takes a heart that is continually grateful to remain connected to the divine.

The continuous flow of the supernatural is maintained by gratitude. Whenever we live our lives with gladness because we know that God is still in control, we keep our doors open for Him to help us again and again. A heart of gratitude helps us keep our joy, despite seemingly impossible situations. It helps keep hope alive and draws upon the wells of strength that lay deep within us. It can transform latent strength into an active force that can help change situations.

It keeps joy in its place in the human spirit, and this attracts strength and peace, despite raging storms. *The joy of the LORD is our strength.* Whenever gratitude is in its right place, the springs of joy are not far from reach. Joy helps us draw upon supernatural strength. Indirectly put, gratitude is strength. The psalmist understood this truth: a heart of gratitude helps maintain your joy, and when joy is in place, your heart can sing, though your situations may seem otherwise.

You turned my wailing into dancing; you removed my sackcloth
and clothed me with joy, that my heart may sing to you and not be silent.
O LORD my God, I will give you thanks forever.
—PSALM 30:11-12

You can never draw upon the wells of strength without some joy within you. It is amazing how God grants us His joy when we live our lives in dependence upon Him with our hearts full of gratitude. He then provides us with the ability to draw from the supernatural:

With joy you will draw water from the wells of salvation.
—ISAIAH 12:3

Words Full of Life

A story is told about one sick man named Lazarus who hailed from a town called Bethany. He had been sick for a while before word came to Jesus about his condition. We are not told exactly what was wrong with him; all the scripture tells us is that he got sick to the point of death and that he died eventually. By the time Jesus got there, Lazarus had been dead for four days.

By the tomb of Lazarus, the apostle John gives us insight into the condition of Christ's heart. His heart was one that was always filled with gratitude. Christ Jesus was enabled to perform the miracle He did because God was with Him. God helped Jesus because in all His actions, He recognised and appreciated His union with the Father. Jesus totally depended upon God as Mediator. By the tomb of Lazarus, Jesus' lips gave expression to what has always been in His heart. Then Jesus looked up and said:

"Father, I thank you that you have heard me. I knew that you always hear me, but I said this for the benefit of the people standing here, that they may believe that you sent me."

—John 11:41-42

Christ, during His days on earth, was heard by His Father because of His reverent fear and submission to the heavenly Father. He spoke and His words had power because His heart was rightly conditioned before God. God empowered His words because His heart was right with Him; He always had a heart full of gratitude. God is looking for human vessels to use for His glory. Every thankful heart is a candidate for God's use.

For when he received honor and glory from God the Father, and the voice was borne to him by the Majestic Glory,
"This is my beloved Son, with whom I am well pleased."

—2 Peter 1:17

Christ Jesus was a man who met this condition, no wonder His words always carried life. Every man who has been truly used by God to lift others up through spoken words has been a man full of gratitude. Life is found in the speech of the grateful. Ungrateful people are full of poison, and they, therefore, 'kill' and destroy. Miracles are in the speech of the grateful. This explains why those who appreciate little things are very good at encouraging others – there is life in their speech.

CHAPTER SIX
True Wholeness

*"True happiness is to enjoy the present, without anxious
dependence upon the future, not to amuse ourselves with either
hopes or fears but to rest satisfied with what we have, which is
sufficient, for he that is so wants nothing. The greatest blessings
of mankind are within us and within our reach. A wise man is
content with his lot, whatever it may be, without wishing for what
he has not."*
—Seneca

The Stages of Life

To be made whole is to be made complete. Wholeness
has to do with being entire, in the fullness of the word.
It is completeness, not just in the body, but also in the
spirit. Whatever God does, He does it in stages. The earth
and everything on it was brought into being in stages;
everything did not appear at once. It is said that 'Rome was
not built in a day.' Every building is built in stages. Ideally,
nobody should place a roof on a house without ensuring
that a solid foundation is in place. Nothing great in life
springs up 'out of the blue'. Everything is first built upon
something else. Restoration in life is, likewise, undertaken
in stages. When the proper order is not followed, disaster
and, therefore, a loss will ensue.

The God of heaven has great plans for all of us, and these
plans are set to occur in stages. Every baby goes through
developmental stages of growth. No baby born with teeth is

a normal baby. God enables a baby to have control of his or her head before He enables the baby to walk. Our wounds are also programmed to heal in stages. This is how God has planned things; God blesses in stages, and He restores wholeness in stages too.

Gratitude and Restoration

A story is told about a group of ten lepers who were blessed to meet Jesus of Nazareth as He later made His way to Jerusalem. These unfortunate ones had been ostracised from society because of leprosy. It was required of those with leprosy to stay away from the general public because the disease was contagious. The lepers were, therefore, found on the outskirts of towns and villages. These lepers had virtually accepted their lot in this life until they heard about the Messiah, who was empowered to change their fortunes.

It was rumoured amongst them that Jesus, after whom the masses thronged, had power to cleanse leprosy. The lepers took advantage of this rare opportunity and dared to approach Jesus and the throng, knowing they were risking their very lives. Standing a long way off, they bid Christ with a loud voice to have mercy on them.

When Christ saw them, He did not condemn them. He asked them to go immediately and present themselves to the priests. In those days, if a leper thought his leprosy was cured, it was mandatory for the priest to clear him and present him with a clearance certificate before he would be accepted back into society. For these ones, who had spent years ostracised from society, they would not want to waste any further time away from their loved ones.

On their way to the priest, they realised that their skin had been cleansed. One of them, noticing what had happened, immediately turned back to seek after Jesus who had been of such immense benevolence to him. He was not ungrateful to wait until the priest had confirmed his healing. He saw his wholeness, restoration and acceptance into society from afar and embraced it with the arms of gratitude.

> *Now faith is being sure of what we hope for and certain of what we do not see.*
>
> —HEBREWS 11:1-2 NIV

There is no act stronger than faith, and there is no faith greater than gratitude for today's little mercies. It is a fact that many lepers who thought their leprosy had been cleansed, occasionally ended up with disappointment when the priest told them they had not been truly cured. The clearing of a leper's skin is a sign that something good had started, but it was never a guarantee that they were completely or truly healed. Men and women of faith do confess by their actions of gratitude that they are a strange breed, unlike the ordinary people.

> *Having seen them afar off were assured of them, embraced them and confessed that they were strangers and pilgrims on the earth*
>
> —HEBREWS 11:13

The stranger in the above story was more than grateful that at least there was evidence to show that something had happened to his skin. Unlike the other nine, he was grateful for little mercies. Though he had not yet been certified and restored to society, at least there was reason for him to be excited; there was something positive about his situation today. His skin now looked clear!

One of them, when he saw he was healed, came back, praising God in a loud voice. He threw himself at Jesus' feet and thanked him-and he was a Samaritan.
—Luke 17:15-16-NIV

Gratitude for small things speaks to God louder than any prayer you can make. It is truly a loud 'cry for attention'. The Samaritans were seen as outsiders and, therefore, strangers to the covenants of promise that the Jews had with Jehovah. This Samaritan did what was not really expected of him since he was a stranger and, therefore, not bound to understand the grace that abounds to those who show gratitude in little things. Jesus was so surprised that those who should have returned to show gratitude did not do so.

Jesus asked, "Were not all ten cleansed? Where are the other nine?
Was no one found to return and give praise to God except this foreigner?"
—LUKE 17:17-19-NIV

Salvation, in all its multifaceted forms, really was initially the preserve of the Jews. Christ Jesus was sent primarily to the 'lost sheep of Israel'. To them belonged the promises that God had made to the patriarchs. The Old Testament prophets saw the Jews as a light to this dark world. They were supposed to not only produce the Messiah but also show the heathen the ways of the true God.

This act of appreciation by the Samaritan opened the door for more mercies to be multiplied to him and for more grace to abound unto him. By his act of gratitude, he had positioned himself for God to quickly move him into the next stage of his healing, the stage of wholeness. The first stage of the restoration was that of cleansing. All ten lepers had been cleansed, but only the grateful one went on into wholeness. The foreigner, by this act, shows us how we position ourselves for the next stage of God's blessing by gratitude.

Gratitude is an act of faith, faith in the Lord, who had started the healing and restoration process, who we trust, that He will surely complete it. God restores in stages, and He heals in stages.

If we want to see the next stage of what God has started to do, we had better be grateful for the little we see Him do in our lives daily. This is the light that section of the Bible sheds upon our hearts, and it was the cleansed Jews who were expected to teach all of us, but they failed to do so by their ingratitude.

> *There are not found that returned to give glory to God, save this stranger.*
> *And he said unto him, Arise, go thy way: thy faith hath made thee whole.*
> —LUKE 17:18-19-KJV

If you truly have faith in God, it will show in your gratitude because true gratitude is true faith in action. Whenever faith is activated, grace comes to our aid.

CHAPTER SEVEN
Activating Grace

*"Gratitude is not only the greatest of virtues, but the parent of all
the others."*
—CICERO

Gratitude Opens the Door to Grace

GRACE IS THE KINDNESS AND love of God to man, accorded
to us on the grounds of God's mercy and not our works of
righteousness. Grace is not just favour, it is the empowering
of Jehovah. **Gratitude opens the door for grace and allows
goodness to come our way.**

> *"He who sacrifices thank offerings honors me, and he
> prepares the way so that I may show him the salvation
> of God."*
> —Psalm 50:23-*NIV*

Without gratitude, grace becomes an outsider who will not
come to you without an invitation to do so. Gratitude is an
indirect invitation for intervention, even in areas you are
not aware that you need help. Gratitude opens the door to
grace because it is no ordinary act; it is a special ministration
to God and man.

Ministration of Gratitude

A minister is a person who serves another: he is a subordinate,
an attendant and one who offers a service which others
may not be qualified to offer. The word 'minister', which

is *Hupeeretes* (Greek), is a greater man's personal attendant. Every true minister is an honoured servant because he or she plays an honoured role. A minister attends upon a superior!

It is the role the minister plays that honors him or her. The servant of a great man is also great because he ministers to the great. This place of privilege is the preserve of just a few. In times past people were specifically chosen and prepared for this office, the ministry of thanksgiving.

The Privileged Levites

The Levites were descendants of Aaron, Israel's first high priest. These people were ministers who were trained to oversee the operations in God's house and to lead the people before God in worship. These descendants of Levi were honoured, in their service to God and their fellow men. It is known that when the ark of God was restored to Israel, King David actually selected certain men to minister before it.

They brought the ark of God's presence and set it inside the tent that David had pitched for it, and they presented burnt offerings and fellowship offerings before God. In addition to these, they also ministered gratitude, gratitude for God's boundless love and mercy.

> *He appointed some of the Levites to minister before the ark of the LORD, to make petition, to give thanks, and to praise the LORD, the God of Israel: Asaph was the chief, Zechariah second, then Jeiel, Shemiramoth, Jehiel, Mattithiah, Eliab, Benaiah, Obed-Edom and Jeiel.*
> —1 CHRONICLES 16: 1, 4-5

*David left Zadok the priest and his fellow priests before
the tabernacle of the LORD at the high place in Gibeon to
present burnt offerings to the LORD on the altar of burnt
offering regularly, morning and evening, in accordance
with everything written in the Law of the LORD, which he
had given Israel. With them were Heman and Jeduthun
and the rest of those chosen and designated by name to
give thanks to the LORD, "for his love endures forever."*
—1 Chronicles 16:39-41

King Hezekiah of the ancient tribe of Judah also understood
that the ministration of the Levites was incomplete without
gratitude.

*Hezekiah assigned the priests and Levites to divisions—
each of them according to their duties as priests or
Levites—to offer burnt offerings and fellowship offerings,
to minister, to give thanks and to sing praises at the gates
of the LORD's dwelling.*
—2 CHRONICLES 31:2-3-NIV

He who has true gratitude does himself a lot of good. He
positions himself for great blessing by indirectly offering
a ministration that pleases God. Every truly thankful soul
indirectly worships God through their acts of gratitude.
Heartfelt gratitude is silent worship. Gratitude is a priestly
act; it completely changes our position spiritually and places
us in a position of blessing.

A True Battle Cry

Gratitude is also a strong battle cry. It is the shout that sends
the army jubilantly onto the battlefield. It is a sign that
shows that we are now ready to face our adversaries. It is
a cry that discomfits our enemies by throwing them into

confusion. It is a sure sign of an invitation for God's help against both our seen and unseen enemies. Without this cry, no army should venture onto the battlefield believing that Jehovah will be on their side. It is that which gathers the masses and grants them the confidence that the battle will be won. Gratitude is the cry for God's mercy; it is a cry based on reliance on God's strength and protection. It is a shout of assurance that God will reach out and save his inheritance.

> *Praise be to the LORD, for he has heard my cry for mercy. The LORD is my strength and my shield; my heart trusts in him, and I am helped.*
> *My heart leaps for joy and I will give thanks to him in song.*
> *The LORD is the strength of his people, a fortress of salvation for his anointed one.*
> *Save your people and bless your inheritance; be their shepherd and carry them forever.*
> —PSALM 28:6-9

The Three-Stranded Attacks

> *Though one may be overpowered, two can defend themselves.*
> *A cord of three strands is not quickly broken.*
> —ECCLESIASTES 4:12

One of the great kings who ruled the ancient kingdom of Judah was King Jehoshaphat. He learnt a lot from the mistakes of his father, King Asa. Despite the mistakes he made, Jehoshaphat was credited with instituting religious reforms in Judah. He learnt one important secret: to lean upon God when things went very wrong.

In the days when Jehoshaphat reigned in Judah, a 'three-banded army' made up of the Moabites, Ammonites and the men of Mount Seir came against him. All of Judah went into panic, for they knew their strength could not march that of this 'unbreakable' force. Jehoshaphat knew exactly where to turn, to the temple of the Lord. In those times, the temple in Jerusalem was a symbol of the presence of the Lord. There, in the forecourt of the temple, in his hour of dire need, Jehoshaphat prayed to the Lord:

> "O LORD, God of our fathers, are you not the God who is in heaven? You rule over all the kingdoms of the nations. Power and might are in your hand, and no one can withstand you. O our God, did you not drive out the inhabitants of this land before your people Israel and give it forever to the descendants of Abraham your friend? They have lived in it and have built in it a sanctuary for your Name, saying, 'If calamity comes upon us, whether the sword of judgment, or plague or famine, we will stand in your presence before this temple that bears your Name and will cry out to you in our distress, and you will hear us and save us.'
>
> "But now here are men from Ammon, Moab and Mount Seir, whose territory you would not allow Israel to invade when they came from Egypt; so they turned away from them and did not destroy them. See how they are repaying us by coming to drive us out of the possession you gave us as an inheritance. O our God, will you not judge them? **For we have no power to face this vast army that is attacking us. We do not know what to do, but our eyes are upon you.**"
>
> All the men of Judah, with their wives and children and little ones, stood there before the LORD.

Then the Spirit of the LORD came upon Jahaziel son of Zechariah, the son of Benaiah, the son of Jeiel, the son of Mattaniah, a Levite and descendant of Asaph, as he stood in the assembly.

He said: "Listen, King Jehoshaphat and all who live in Judah and Jerusalem! This is what the LORD says to you: 'Do not be afraid or discouraged because of this vast army. For the battle is not yours, but God's.
Tomorrow march down against them. They will be climbing up by the Pass of Ziz, and you will find them at the end of the gorge in the Desert of Jeruel. You will not have to fight this battle. Take up your positions; stand firm and see the deliverance the LORD will give you, O Judah and Jerusalem. Do not be afraid; do not be discouraged. **Go out to face them tomorrow***, and the LORD will be with you.'"*

—2 CHRONICLES 20:6-17 (EMPHASIS MINE)

One great secret in life is to take life a day at a time and to face life with gratitude. You may be facing an army of storms and battles; learn to relax, and tomorrow's battle will be dealt with when you get there. To face tomorrow's storms, you need a gratitude mentality. You may not be where you want to be today, but you should learn to embrace tomorrow with gratitude.

The king and the entire army slept that night and woke up the following day and marched out to face the so-called invincible three-stranded army. Their style and military strategy are noteworthy:

Early in the morning they left for the Desert of Tekoa. As they set out, Jehoshaphat stood and said, "Listen to me, Judah and people of Jerusalem! Have faith in the

LORD your God and you will be upheld; have faith in his prophets and you will be successful." After consulting the people, Jehoshaphat appointed men to sing to the LORD and to praise him for the splendor of his holiness as they went out at the head of the army, saying:
"Give thanks to the LORD,
for his love endures forever."
As they began to sing and praise with grateful hearts, the LORD set ambushes against the men of Ammon and Moab and Mount Seir who were invading Judah, and they were defeated.

—2 CHRONICLES 20:20-22

In the face of imminent battle, there was still a song of gratitude in their hearts. The king and his army marched onto the field of battle with songs of gratitude and praise. This discomfited the three-stranded offensive of the enemy. It brought down the omnipotence of God to fight a seemingly invincible army. This army of mortal men attracted the immortal power of the highest by the channel of thankful praise.

This is the reality in the natural. This explains why the truly thankful may have several challenges, but they still pull through all of them. These thankful people do not rely on their own strength; they know they have very little strength. Their grateful hearts supernaturally draw upon the power of the highest. It is a fact that most of the deprived people in our world live in the third world. They have mountain loads of challenges, yet they survive all of these, I believe, because many of them have hearts full of gratitude for little mercies. Unknown to them, their gratitude draws in grace to face their obstacles. Any rational person will truly question how these deprived people make it. Many people believe that it is the poor who need God.

These poor people apply certain basic principles which do work for them.

How true it is that he who sacrifices thanks offerings honours God, and he prepares the way so that God may show him His salvation (Psalm 50:23). When we truly give thanks, despite all our dire needs, we directly invite God's omnipotence to fight our impending battles. Praiseful thanks are true, faithful praise. Spiritually, it always discomfits the invading enemy.

Through faithful praise, you, too, can be named among those, *who through faith conquered kingdoms, administered justice, and gained what was promised; who shut the mouths of lions, quenched the fury of the flames, and escaped the edge of the sword; whose weakness was turned to strength; and who became powerful in battle and routed foreign armies* (Hebrews 11:33–35).

CHAPTER EIGHT
Ignoramus

"Only a stomach that rarely feels hungry scorns common things."
—HORACE

Ignorance Blinds and Enslaves

MANY PEOPLE DO NOT VALUE some simple things in life because they are so common to them. An ignorant person is not only one who lacks knowledge but also one who lacks information, which may be simple, but yet, very vital. An ignoramus is an individual who is not well informed on an issue. Abundance can truly be costly and blinding. One may be educated in one field and very ignorant in many other areas. This is a common reality.

There can be a vast difference between truth and reality. Reality is what we see and experience, which could be very different from the truth. An individual may appear very privileged, yet in reality, he may be potentially very sick within: the problem may simply be ignorance of what truly matters in life.

Ignorance enslaves; it puts shackles on men, rendering them virtually impotent. Because of lack of knowledge of what life is all about, great men have condescended to poverty of the heart and have never found the place of true fulfilment in life. They keep chasing after all manner of things in life and only when they come close to their death do they realise that they have run a wrong race. Ignorance of some basic truths has the ability to easily convince us that all we see is all there is in our situation.

An individual may not have all the material blessings many yearn for but may be in the best of spiritual health and emotional well-being. Ignorance of fundamental truth blindfolds its victims and can make potential 'princes' envy the 'privileged' poor. When we fail to realize that we are truly blessed to have the basic necessities of life, we will walk around envying everybody else as we chase after material things without appreciating the many free blessings all around us.

Wandering Royalty

Ignorance deceives and humiliates eventually. There is no greater slavery than walking through life ignorant of how blessed you are and what you can really achieve with a grateful attitude. When men live without gratitude, they will fail to discover who they truly are, and they wander away from the fullness of their intended and planned destiny. A wanderer does not know where he is headed. Wanderers often look and feel wretched in the natural. There are also those who appear to have made it, but they are really a mess within because they do not appreciate the many little blessings in their lives. They are very unhappy within because they are ungrateful at heart.

> *"Happiness is itself a kind of gratitude."*
> —JOSEPH WOOD KRUTCH

Ungrateful souls lack true dignity and honour and hardly win respect from the truly simple and noble. A wanderer is like a stray dog that has no home to return to. It eats from every place and never has the peace of what one will call the safety and peace of a home. He eats without joy, and his predisposition for more and more leaves him wretched from within. Ungrateful souls may appear to have plenty, yet they are always lusting for more of what belongs to others.

Without gratitude, men who were born to become 'noble' eventually wander into the wilderness of this life. Ingratitude is, in reality, a shade of rebellion. An ungrateful person is not different from the rebellious at heart; they are the same people 'singing' a different song.

A Rebellious Heart

Most rebellious people are very ungrateful people. A sign of ingratitude is complete severance from those who have helped them. They are individuals who believe everyone owes them something but forget the good that others have done for them too. They are selfish people who go out for one thing: self-gratification now. They know no delayed gratification but seek immediate joy, damning the consequences of their actions. They fail to appreciate who they are, and they even end up envying those who are, in reality, less privileged than they are. Ungrateful people feel they are entitled to everything.

Men who show little gratitude to the Almighty Creator cannot show respect and appreciation to their fellow men. Like the prodigal son, they feel they are entitled to so much. They wander from the place that is supposed to be their real home and identify with mediocrity. They eventually get to the point where they even desire 'pig feed'. In their wandering, they begin to die slowly but surely. By their ingratitude, they end up hiring themselves to do 'menial' jobs, even though they are royalty.

Ungrateful people, like every other rebellious person, cannot find true peace and fulfilment. They try to fill up the void within them with wild living, other activities and achievements, but these can never really bring them lasting joy. Unless the ungrateful come to their senses, they will remain slaves and, therefore, unfulfilled wanderers for life.

Make Us like Them

One of the sure signs of ingratitude is to want to be like others.

Ingratitude is showing gross dissatisfaction in how we were created and who we are. Ungrateful people do not appreciate their worth but see good in others. They adore every other person but themselves. They are ignorant about who they really are and what they can achieve. They are therefore lost in our world, and they grope in the deep darkness of ignorance, singing the praises of others.

The 'Akans' of Ghana say that it is a curse to wish to be like another. It is very unwise to judge an individual just by what our limited eyes perceive. It is a truth that the eyes can only see what the eyes have been engineered to see. We are so limited in what we are allowed to know about others from a distance. Yet we live our lives with impressions made from what we see and perceive about others.

Just as the grass always looks greener on the other side, we often see and think others are more privileged than we are. This is life's mirage; it is deception to believe that what you see about others is everything you have always dreamt of. Many times, you are far better off than many of those you envy. There is no need to wish to be like another person. If you care to know, many of those who daily pray and wish they were like others are more blessed than those they envy. Their problem is basically ignorance. They are ignorant about who they really are and what they possess. How sad that many want to be like others and are not grateful for what God has given them.

The desire to be like others has pushed young girls into prostitution. Wanting to wear expensive clothing and jewellery has driven young ladies into wrong company. Their lives have been influenced negatively as they have been enticed by the lure of a supposedly easy life into a life of bondage to sex and immorality. Some young men and women have followed the attractions of glamour and glitz into the underworld of hard drug addictions. Greed for more money has sent men and women of great potential behind bars for embezzling money from their employers.

Some have been trapped in the trade of drug trafficking. They cannot come out of it because they are hooked to this trade. Many others have come under the influence of dark and evil spirits as they have been introduced to all forms of negative vices, including sodomy, bestiality and the use of hard liquor. Young men and women have abandoned school to chase after money. In their haste to get rich quickly, many have died prematurely and pierced themselves with many sorrows.

A King like Theirs

"Gratefulness is the key to a happy life that we hold in our hands, because if we are not grateful, then no matter how much we have we will not be happy — because we will always want to have something else or something more."
—Brother David Steindl-Rast

Many people are unthankful because they do not appreciate

who they are, what they have and how far they can go. As a result of their ignorance, they are bereft of gratitude. Their hearts are plagued with sorrow and envy instead of being flooded with gratitude. They envy others and wish they could have what others have. They blame their inadequacy on others and the systems around them. They believe others are successful because of what and who they have in their camp.

It is important to realise that a king is only as strong as his subjects. The true worth of any group of people is not just in their leadership, it is in the people themselves. It is the people who make the king who he is. No matter how good a leader is, he cannot achieve much without the common folk.

When the common folk have an identity crises, they will fail, even if God came in the flesh to lead them. How often we have been deceived into thinking that our lot would be different only if we had what others have. *If only we had a leader like theirs. If only the management board was changed. If only I had a different husband. If only I had what the other person got…*

These and several similar sentiments run through the minds of many people who are very dissatisfied with their lot in life. These people fail to realise that true victory begins from within them. They fail to see that no matter what you get into your life, whether it is leadership, counsel or material things, your victory starts when you discover yourself and begin to work your situation out from within. It begins with an awareness of self.

A realistic assessment of who you are, what you have and what you can do is victory in itself. If you have to change anything or anybody in your life, first change yourself and your mindset. You think your husband or wife is not good, ask yourself first if you are good enough. No matter how bad a leader or team player may be, your best bet is not to change them. Your best bet for change is yourself. Wrong mindsets produce negative patterns and attitudes, which lead to repeated incidences of defeat. True defeat begins from deep within us; it is not just because of those around or over us. Every change made around us becomes more effective and profitable when it is matched with positive changes within us.

We all have battles to fight on an individual basis daily. We can only do well when we have peace within and we look up to God to strengthen us. To truly tap into the grace and strength of God, we need to be focused and determined. When we are so engrossed in the lives of others and what they have or what seems to be an advantage they may have over us, we cannot be effective in our daily battles. To focus on the non-essentials is to lose the battle for the essentials of life. The secret or revealed desire to be or have what the others may have will blind your eyes to the manifold blessings God has bequeathed to you.

The Ignorant Masses

There are many today who do not see how privileged they are, even in their humble circumstances. Millions of people take so many things for granted. They believe they are entitled to the basic necessities of life: water, shelter, food and electricity. These ones should be reminded that there are several million human beings like them who lack these basic necessities because they 'committed the crime' of being born unprivileged and into a home with a 'wrong' address.

Gratitude is not being thankful for what you do not deserve, it is being thankful even for what you believe you are entitled to. Grateful people know that in this unfair world they may not really be entitled to anything at all. They understand that what they have and who they are is still attributable to providence and not just their human efforts.

> *"Do not keep talking so proudly or let your mouth speak such arrogance, for the LORD is a God who knows, and by him deeds are weighed.*
> *"The bows of the warriors are broken, but those who stumbled are armed with strength.*
> *Those who were full hire themselves out for food, but those who were hungry hunger no more.*
> *She who was barren has borne seven children, but she who has had many sons pines away.*
> *"The LORD brings death and makes alive; he brings down to the grave and raises up.*
> *The LORD sends poverty and wealth; he humbles and he exalts.*
> *He raises the poor from the dust and lifts the needy from the ash heap; he seats them with princes and has them inherit a throne of honor."*
> —1 SAMUEL 2:3-8-NIV

She Acquired a Greedy Eye

There is a story I chanced upon about a young lady who got married and was happy until they moved into a flat in the city. Their new neighbours were also a young couple who appeared to be well to do. As this young lady spent time with the neighbours, she gradually began to envy what her friend had. On the outside, it appeared as if she and her husband were just making ends meet and their neighbours were really enjoying a life of abundance.

She soon started envying her friend who seemed to have all the nice clothes, jewellery and a lot of cash to spread around. Her friend's flat also looked better furnished than theirs, and she began to yearn for those things. This soon started affecting her own marriage as she spent more time at her friend's place to the detriment of her husband's needs. This was followed by open disrespect for her husband, and she would cast slurring insinuations at her husband at the least opportunity.

With time, she stopped going to church and started partying wildly with her worldly friends. She was deceived by the neighbour's wife to divorce her husband, and she left her matrimonial home and her small daughter behind. This brought severe pain and pressure to her husband whose condition had been worsened by losing his job after his company folded up. The lady was introduced to a handsome young man by her worldly friend and soon was remarried to this rich, flamboyant, young man who claimed to be a businessman.

Many years later, some armed robbers were arrested in a police swoop, and her businessman husband was one of them. She ended up with nothing but shame and regret. Not all that glitters is gold. Look into your own pot and not that of your neighbour. Greed and envy will not take you far.

CHAPTER NINE
The Dance of the Lord

*"Some people have a wonderful capacity to appreciate again
and again, freshly and naively, the basic goods of life, with awe,
pleasure, wonder, and even ecstasy."*
—A.H. MASLOW

An Exuberant Spirit

Where true gratitude exists, life is never absent. Grateful
people are often exuberant souls. These are individuals
with very lively spirits. Their glow is often infectious; they
spread life and hope wherever they find themselves. There
is a fountain of life flowing from deep within them that
affects everything they do and everyone they meet. They
are often at peace with themselves and with their God. It
does not take long for one to realise that there is some grace
upon their lives.

They indirectly minister life to all who come their way.
God is pleased to use such people because they can represent
Him excellently. They are almost always hopeful and warm
souls who have learnt the secret of inner peace and joy.
Grateful souls exude life even when they smile. Everything
they touch is quickened, and they have what it takes to

resurrect 'dead' and despondent souls. It is often a joy to be around these 'special' ones. They are special because they live as if they had no sorrows and very little worries.

Grateful souls have mastered the art of allowing the springs of joy and life within them to influence every other thing around them. They know the force and power of inner strength that results from contentment.

Youthful Souls

True gratitude keeps our souls 'young'. It helps us to keep the joy of youthfulness. That childlike liberty and faith that believes in all kinds of possibilities is ignited by gratitude. It enables one to have the bright innocence of childhood and produces inner liberation. It has a therapeutic effect upon our spirits, causing the release of chemicals within our system that keeps us feeling young and lively.

It not only enlivens our hearts, but it brightens our faces: its effects are seen outwardly. A heart full of gratitude can slow down the ageing process, reduce the rate of skin wrinkling and even hasten wound healing. It speeds up healing among the sick, and it may help delay deteriorating processes in our physical bodies. True gratitude can help you fight diseases. Somehow, it primes your immune system to fight against disease. Generally speaking, grateful souls even live longer, all things being equal.

When the Heart Sings

It is a fact that no matter how depraved a man's heart may be, every now and then, even the depraved heart sings. When the heart of man is excited, melodies spring out from within it. Gratitude conditions the heart to sing. It primes the heart, excites it and, consequently, songs flow from within. Every merry heart sings, and a singing heart radiates life and energy into the whole system. This positive energy energises our whole system and makes us dance on the inside.

It is a truth that a man may be going through all kinds of storms and still be at peace. It is also a truth that a man's life can seem plagued with all kinds of storms, yet he could be dancing deep within himself.

Gratitude keeps our hearts dancing shoes within reach. It promises us that we could still partake of a victory dance within us, no matter what happens on the outside. Deep gratitude makes the heart leap from within. It ushers us into a realm and domain of supernatural strength. It shifts our focus from the natural into the supernatural. When the heart sings from deep within, the feet ultimately respond with a dance. In this state, you also begin to dance, even in the physical realm under the influence of God's Spirit.

During this dance, men are seen for who they really are in relation to God: frail, mere mortals. You will notice, then, that the dance you are dancing is extraordinary. All 'pride' crumbles and shame flees, and some godly boldness takes over. This is the same kind of dance the historical King David danced when the ark of God was returned to its abode in Jerusalem.

> *As the ark of the LORD was entering the City of David, Michal daughter of Saul watched from a window. And when she saw King David leaping and dancing before the LORD, she despised him in her heart.*
> —2 SAMUEL 6:16-NIV

This explains exactly what was happening to the King; he was dancing 'before the Lord'. Something on the inside must have been stirred up because this was an extraordinary dance. The cords of deep gratitude had been struck, and the wells of joy set into motion. He looked quite ridiculous before mere mortals; he was not himself. The Spirit of God had taken over and ushered him into the 'very presence of God'. He had entered another realm and was expressing another form of gratitude before God through dance.

The New King James version of the Bible tells us that the grateful king was not just taking amazing, extraordinary leaps, he was whirling all over the place, as if he was the blade of a propeller. Obviously, he was excited beyond himself. He just could not control himself, though he might have attempted to do so initially. The inner force of gratitude just could not be silenced; his spirit responded with an extraordinary dance. Gratitude excites us into a real celebration.

This dance was pleasing before God because it was a response of true gratitude. This was a man of high aristocratic rank who was neither ashamed nor offended by a public display of gratitude to God. It is not surprising that David is referred to in the Bible as a man after the heart of God. When David's wife attempted to chide him because of this, he silenced her immediately saying:

> "It was before the LORD, who chose me instead of your father and all his house, to appoint me ruler over the people of the LORD, over Israel.
> Therefore I will play music before the LORD. And I will be even more undignified than this, and will be humble in my own sight."
>
> —2 Samuel 6:21-22-NKJV

David knew too well that it was only divine providence that had bequeathed him with a throne he really did not deserve. He knew that God had handpicked him from the backside of the wilderness and elevated him. He had been leapfrogged from the status of a common shepherd to an exemplary king. His gratitude was beyond bounds; why would he not dance? He knew how far he had come by the grace of the Lord, and this, he would never forget.

> *Then King David went in and sat before the LORD, and he said:*
> *"Who am I, O Sovereign LORD, and what is my family, that you have brought me this far? And as if this were not enough in your sight, O Sovereign LORD, you have also spoken about the future of the house of your servant. Is this your usual way of dealing with man, O Sovereign LORD?"*
> —2 SAMUEL 7:18-19-NIV

God was pleased with King David but very displeased with Michal (David's wife) for despising a man who attempted to say thank you through an unorthodox dance. So displeased was He with David's wife Michal that her womb was shut as a result. She was not permitted to bring 'her kind' into the world. She died childless because she failed to appreciate true gratitude and had little respect for men of honour who knew the value of true gratitude. David lived long and reigned as the greatest king in Israel's history. He was empowered to do many great things for Israel and God.

The Deformed Dancer

I once travelled for a funeral in rural Ghana a few years

ago. I remember it as if it was just yesterday. Funerals in our part of the world are get-together occasions for family and friends. It is often one of the few occasions that bring people together to rejuvenate and catch up with friends and families for the long periods we have not seen each other. One of the highlights of these funerals was the food and drinks that are normally shared and enjoyed by everyone present.

At this particular funeral, a young man had passed, and I travelled to support a friend who was related to the deceased. There were a group of teenage boys who, after having scrambled for a handful meal, started dancing their hearts out in the open to highlife music. These young boys formed a circle and took turns to entertain the crowd by entering the centre of the circle to dance to the cheering of their colleagues and the crowd. A young boy who might have suffered from polio took his turn, and it was amazing what he could do with his right leg, which was deformed and shorter. He had so much joy within, and he danced as if he had no troubles in his life. He was so cheerful, even off the dancing floor, and I later got to know that he was an orphan and a shoemaker.

This young man had suffered from polio in his childhood, and this had resulted in a deformed right leg. Both of his parents were dead and gone, and he had to make ends meet at a very young age with no relative to help. He had no education and no siblings, yet he was cheerful. He could have been bitter and angry with everyone, including his parents, family and friends, yet he was cheerful at heart. Even for lunch, he had to scramble with his friends to get a morsel, yet he was not bitter with everybody.

He could have been ashamed and even timid because of

his deformity, but he was a free, lively and grateful soul, thankful for the little things he had going for him. He was deformed in one leg, but he was not deformed at heart. He was grateful at heart that he was alive that day. He was happy for his friends around him and glad that there was a social gathering with music that cheered his heart. He had a dancing heart, and his feet responded to the rhythm within, first and foremost, even before he heard the high life song. How true the saying that when your heart is right, indeed, your feet will dance.

There are many who may not have a deformity, yet they are not grateful for all the blessings they have received from the hands of the invisible God who lives forever. We all need to sit and count our blessings and develop a heart of gratitude towards God for all His great mercies. May we all, with gratitude for all God has done for us and brought us through, put on our dancing shoes and dance in celebration.

God has indeed been good, and He is good to those who show gratitude for little mercies. Anytime you are sad and down, remember the deformed, young man who danced as if he had no troubles. If he can dance, then you too, should learn to do the same. God will give all grateful souls an inner song that will keep our hearts strong and our feet nimble. Put on your dancing shoes, and let heaven know you are thankful. Yes, you too can let heaven know that you are truly very, very grateful for everything.

CHAPTER TEN
Resurrection Power

For land that has drunk the rain that often falls on it, and produces a crop useful to those for whose sake it is cultivated...
—HEBREWS 6:7

Open up for Spring Season

THE EARTH'S ABILITY TO RECEIVE rain that falls upon it is what permits it to receive new life after a season of dryness. It has to drink of the rain that falls from above before any produce can come out of it. Every spring we see new life all around us. The fields become green again, the birds come out to chirp and all the animals that had gone into hibernation come out of their long periods of rest. The cows are seen on the hillside, which has become grassy after the early spring rains.

All these are possible because the earth has the capacity to receive the blessing of the Lord. Those who walk and live their lives with gratitude have the ability to receive and produce new life. Gratitude is the desire, the thirst and the hunger for God to visit the dry places of your life with His rain.

When we live with hearts filled with gratitude for God's mercies, he enlarges our life in due season. You will be given the power to endure the long and difficult seasons of your life. He will send His angels to keep you, and your tired arms He will strengthen. They will fortify you to run the journey ahead of you.

Gratitude will preserve your soul to endure the wintery seasons of life. Soon you will embrace the strength that comes from above to help you recuperate from the barraging dry winds of the past challenging months. Your portion will soon embrace the early spring sprout. Gratitude invites new life. When we show gratitude to God, we honour the great provider, and out of His benevolence, He will quench our dry and parched lands.

> *The wild beasts will honor me, the jackals and the ostriches, for I give water in the wilderness, rivers in the desert, to give drink to my chosen people whom I formed for myself that they might declare my praise.*
> —ISAIAH 43:20

Grateful Souls

> *And Jesus lifted up his eyes and said, "Father, I thank you that you have heard me. I knew that you always hear me, but I said this on account of the people standing around, that they may believe that you sent me."*
> —JOHN 11:41B

Jesus Christ was successful on His earthly mission because He had a heart of gratitude at all times. The above discourse at the graveside of Lazarus gives us insight into this truth. He knew that the Father always heard Him, and He was always thankful. We shall consider some truths from John chapter eleven.

1. *Inner Peace in Time of Distress*

   Grateful souls have peace, even in the midst of chaos. Jesus Christ had inner peace, even though He was informed that His friend Lazarus had fallen ill. Despite this early information, He stayed two days longer in the place where He was (John 11:5-6).

2. *Inner Light*

   Grateful souls have light within them. Christ was aware later that Lazarus was dead by virtue of the inner light within him. He was prepared to travel to Judea, even though previously He had been a wanted man in Judea. By the inner light, He became aware that the situation in Judea had changed, and He could now safely travel there.

3. *Optimism*

   Grateful souls are optimistic. By virtue of the inner light, Christ was aware that Lazarus' sickness was not supposed to end in death. Lazarus had just fallen asleep. As such, even after Jesus perceived that His friend had now passed, He was still optimistic that the heavenly Father was going to raise him up from the grave.

4. *Outward Aura*

   Grateful souls have an aura around them that keeps destruction away. Martha said to Jesus, "Lord, if you had been here my brother would not have died. Mary reiterated this message when she fell at Christ's feet.

"Lord, if you had been here, my brother would not have died."

5. *Empathetic Soul*

Grateful souls are empathetic. Christ stood at the tomb of Lazarus and wept for him (John 11:35).

6. *Agents of Resurrection*

Grateful souls are God's agents of resurrection. Every genuine man sent from God and used by God to prevent unnecessary death has a heart filled with continuous gratitude to God. It should not surprise us that Jesus cried out with a loud voice, *"Lazarus, come out." The man who had died came out, his hands and feet bound with linen strips, and his face wrapped with a cloth. Jesus said to them, "Unbind him, and let him go."*

The Example of the Shunammite Woman

1. *Contentment*

Grateful souls are satisfied with their lot in life. The woman from the town of Shunam understood that one cannot have everything in this sphere. She was rich materially but had no children, yet she was satisfied with her lot. She did not need any favours from any king or commander (2 Kings 4:12-13). She answered, *"I dwell among my own people."*

2. *Benevolence*

Grateful souls are benevolent. The woman from Shunam was benevolent with what she had been blessed with (2 Kings 4:8). She built a room and furnished it with a bed, a table, a chair and a lamp for the prophet Elisha.

3. *Inner Light*

Grateful souls have inner light. The woman from Shunam perceived that Elisha was a holy man of God when she met him (2 Kings 4:9).

4. *Power to Conceive*

Grateful souls receive power to conceive and give birth to the extraordinary. At the season of spring, she conceived and bore a son, even though her husband was old (2 Kings 4:14, 17).

5. *Maintain Inner Peace*

Grateful souls have peace and remain calm, even when under an attack. When the woman of Shunam lost her son, she remained calm and did not fret. She said, *"All is well"* (2 Kings 4:18-23).

6. *Maintain Positive Confession*

Grateful souls have positive or optimistic speech. The woman of Shunam still spoke words of hope, even in the heat of a very difficult test. She said, *"All is well"* (2 Kings 4:23 & 26).

CHAPTER ELEVEN
Delayed and Aborted Promises

For you have need of endurance, so that when you have done the will of God you may receive what is promised.
—HEBREWS 10:36

LIFE IS, INDEED, A CONTINUOUS series of battles. You have not been promised an easy ride, so do not expect one. However, you can choose to go through life with God and with your loved ones by your side. They will offer us the comfort and guidance we need to keep us sane and afloat. In the midst of all life's storms, we will need to keep calm and know how to handle all the pressures that come with the storms. You need endurance to help you brace through the turmoil of life. With endurance and a great attitude, your soul can still flourish despite all the troubles around you.

What have you been thinking about? Are they thoughts of doubt, fear, blame and doom, or are they thoughts of gratitude, faith and bloom? Your thoughts affect your ability to endure the troubles around you. If Apostle Paul had been here today, he would ask you to think thoughts that are true, lovely, pleasant and pure. You need to think about good things if you want to be able to get through storms. When our thought life is wrong, we will have troubled lives. We need to study the word of God to get His guiding principles through life. Our troubles will seek to influence our thoughts, but we need to guide our thoughts to overcome our circumstances. God wants us to be grateful and to walk in faith.

Gratitude and Strength

A mindset of gratitude will influence and invigorate our spirits and make them stout to brace through all the challenges life will throw at us. Gratitude of heart and mind will help you build up endurance and a great outlook on life and its vicissitudes. They will help you deal with the negative messages you never thought would come your way. Gratitude and endurance will help you deal with the enemy's voice that keeps telling you that you deserve to die. They will help you deal with the unanswered questions your heart longs for.

Gratitude for all that God and life has brought you will allow you to build up endurance to help you deal with all the negativity around you. You need both, or you will spend your life chasing after things or trying to be as good as or better than others. Without gratitude, you will not have the staying power to say no to the pressure to be like others. You need power to stand your ground until your change comes. Stop running your life rugged!

Both of these attributes will help you deal with criticism you will face in life. They will help you fight to live to see your children and grandchildren. They will help you see through the eyes of hope. They have the power to shorten the years of your pain and the burden you are carrying.

Gratitude births endurance which will not only see you through the storms but also shorten the years of pain you may have to go through to see your next opportunity for change. They will carry you in their arms and bring you to your next phase of life. Gratitude has a way of shortening our 'night' seasons and ushering us into the day of blessing and opportunity. It will help you deal with all forms of 'wrath' and make your journey look relatively shorter.

> *Sing praises to the LORD, O you his saints, and give thanks to his holy name. For his anger is but for a moment, and his favor is for a lifetime. Weeping may tarry for the night, but joy comes with the morning.*
> —PSALM 30:4-5

Ingratitude and Delays

Thanksgiving can turn a journey that is meant to last for years to appear like a journey of a few months. Gratitude to God for His mercies will make your days of stress and turmoil look like a moment. It also has the ability to 'prolong' your moments of favour to look like a lifetime event. It will not only bring hope, but it helps us go through our night seasons with much more ease. It offers us comfort and strength to endure the season of lack, making it more bearable as we look forward to the season of change just around the corner.

The children of Israel spent 40 days spying on the Promised Land; all but two came back with a bad report. They came back in fear, inciting the rest of the congregation to grumble against God in ingratitude for a 'promised land full of giants'. For grumbling, as a result of the 40 days of not appreciating the mercies and provision of God, that generation spent 40 years in suffering. Grumbling is a sure sign of ingratitude, and it sent them into 40 years of suffering. A journey which should have taken just a few weeks was prolonged to 40 years with suffering for showing ingratitude.

"How long shall this wicked congregation grumble against me? I have heard the grumblings of the people of Israel, which they grumble against me? Say to them, 'As I live, declares the LORD, what you have said in my hearing I will do to you: your dead bodies shall fall in this wilderness and of all your number, listed in the census from twenty years old and upward, who have grumbled against me, not one shall come into the land I swore that I would make you dwell, except Caleb the son of Jephunneh and Joshua the son of Nun. But your little ones, who you said would be prey, I will bring in, and they shall know the land that you rejected. But as for you, your dead bodies shall fall in this wilderness. And your children shall be shepherds in the wilderness forty years and shall suffer for your faithlessness, until the last bodies' lies in the wilderness. According to the number of days in which you spied out the land, forty days, a year for each day, you shall bear your iniquity forty years, and you shall know my displeasure.' I the LORD, have spoken."

—NUMBERS 14:27-35

Oh, how many promises of God we delay and even forfeit because we are ungrateful and faithless. We need to pray for strength to face the giants on our way to the next promise and not grumble and complain about them. As we thank God daily for His manifold blessings we have already seen and continue to enjoy, it becomes easier to look at the challenges ahead with hope, faith and gratitude.

We need to understand that we are prolonging our suffering and battles when we walk in ingratitude and faithlessness. We shorten our suffering and battles indirectly by walking in faith and gratitude to God for His daily mercies. We should see the little God has given us as plenty in anticipation for what He is still doing and shall do for us. Our gratitude needs to be spontaneous and not given when we please. We all need a grateful heart, for then, we shorten our night seasons of trouble and gain acceleration into the day of His boundless abundance.

"Thou that has given so much to me,
Give one thing more—a grateful heart;
Not thankful when it pleaseth me, as if thy blessings had spare
days; But such a heart, whose pulse may be Thy praise."
—GEORGE HERBERT

CHAPTER TWELVE
Empowering the Can-Do Spirit

"Whatever you appreciate and give thanks for will increase in your life."
—SANAYA ROMAN, *LIVING WITH JOY: KEYS TO PERSONAL POWER AND SPIRITUAL TRANSFORMATION*

ALL FIRES NEED SOME FUEL to keep them burning. Fuel is any material burned to produce heat or power. What does any rational individual do to revive a fire that is dying off? They just add more fuel. If they fail to do so, the fire, no matter how important it was, will die with time. Some fires may not be crucial to our existence, others are.

The person of the Holy Spirit produces an extraordinary fire in the heart of the Christian. This inner fire produces the warmth of hopeful assurance and inner peace and makes us believe in all kinds of possibilities. The Holy Spirit is an empowering Spirit from God that Jesus of Nazareth promised that all who believe in Him would receive. The Holy Spirit's fire also needs fuel to burn brightly. His fire can be put off either deliberately or unintentionally.

> *Pray continually, give thanks in all circumstances; for this is God's will for you in Christ Jesus. Do not put out the Spirit's fire.*
> —1 THESSALONIANS 5:17-19-NIV

One of the things that set this fire ablaze is prayer. Others include joy and gladness. Yet another is true gratitude. Yes, genuine gratitude to God ignites the fires of God's Spirit within our hearts.

Stranded on the Highway

In this life, everybody desires to be journeying on a highway called progress. No sound person would wish retrogression or stagnation for himself. It is a truth that no vehicle will move without some form of fuel. No matter how big and powerful your car engine is, it is powerless without fuel. No matter how bright your future may look, you need to make progress to get there. It is only a fool who embarks on a long journey without taking into consideration how he will be able to periodically refill his fuel tank. Remember that the 'biggest' SUV is only as powerful as the fuel its tank carries. Without fuel, the machine is virtually useless!

Believe it or not, your God is only as powerful and big as the amount of 'fuel' you give Him. Your God can only take you as far as the fuel you give Him will last. Without gratitude, you could have a very big God and still be stranded and very immobile on the highway of progress.

The Ungrateful Son

No matter how much a father loves an ungrateful son, he gets to a point when his heart becomes grieved by repeated incidents of ingratitude. Every ungrateful child soon becomes a 'burden' to his father. A 'burdened' man's heart will also be burdened. Ingratitude grieves a father's heart and weakens his desire to be good to an ungrateful son. Ingratitude turns the heart of God against us; it grieves His Spirit. The Holy Spirit is power from on high; He is the empowering force of God. When God's Spirit is excited, He empowers the believer. When He is grieved by ingratitude, His power does not flow into and through our lives.

In similar manner, the father's heart is gladdened by a grateful son. Goodness flows from the heart of an excited father towards his children. A gladdened heart is an empowered heart that makes all things possible. It is truly fuel for His Spirit who dwells within our hearts. Contentment with what we have 'enables' God's Spirit within us.

Releasing the Goodness of God

It is no secret that goodness always flows from God's gladdened heart. His heart has always been gladdened by grateful people. It is true that God is enthroned in the true praises of His people. Many who fail to praise Him are really ungrateful souls. Heartfelt gratitude lifts true praise to God, who responds with goodness unto men.

Enter his gates with thanksgiving and his courts with praise;
give thanks to him and praise his name.
For the LORD is good and his love endures forever; his faithfulness continues through all generations.
—PSALM 100:4-5

Give thanks to the LORD, for he is good.
His love endures forever.
Give thanks to the God of gods.
His love endures forever.
Give thanks to the Lord of lords:
His love endures forever.
—PSALM 136:1-3

The Secret

The apostle Paul, according to Biblical history, achieved so much in his earthly life. He was used so mightily of God to minister God's grace and love to Gentile nations. He operated in so many gifts of grace, including teaching, healing and the miraculous. He faced so many storms and obstacles, yet he braced through all of them. Paul, in his own words, describes just a little of what he went through:

> *In labors more abundant, in stripes above measure, in prisons more frequently, in deaths often. From the Jews five times I received forty stripes minus one. Three times I was beaten with rods; once I was stoned; three times I was shipwrecked; a night and a day I have been in the deep; in journeys often, in perils of waters, in perils of robbers, in perils of my own countrymen, in perils of the Gentiles, in perils in the city, in perils in the wilderness, in perils in the sea, in perils among false brethren; in weariness and toil, in sleeplessness often, in hunger and thirst, in fastings often, in cold and nakedness-- besides the other things, what comes upon me daily: my deep concern for all the churches.*
> —2 CORINTHIANS 11:23-28-NKJV

How did he pull through all of these hurdles? Many who have studied this man's life story do not cease to be amazed at the dramatic turnaround of his life. Even more outstanding was how useful he became as a vessel of grace in God's hands. How was he able to accomplish so much?

Paul picked up a secret key on his way through life. He had a 'secret weapon' he used against all the mountains of problems he faced. This he revealed to the church in Philippi:

I know what it is to be in need, and I know what it is to have plenty. I have learned the secret of being content in any and every situation, whether well fed or hungry, whether living in plenty or in want. I can do everything through him who gives me strength.

—PHILIPPIANS 4:12-13

A heart that was content with its lot no matter the situation was Paul's secret. This condition of his heart made all things possible for him. It enabled the can-do spirit within him. He could boldly say *I can do all things through him who strengthens me.* This was only possible because he learnt to live and walk this earthly journey in contentment.

Contentment also enables and empowers men to do that which is difficult. So often in the valleys of difficulty, we are tempted to want to be like others who, at the moment, may look more 'blessed'. This may not necessarily be so. Envy is unnecessary, especially when you have gratitude as your secret. Gratitude will enable you to love even those who hate you. It will empower you to release that which can make you a slave. It can help break the power of greed from your life.

Contentment will allow you to love God in truth. You will not have to feign love for Him because you need anything from Him. You will begin to understand the frailty of human life and the value of the human soul. Contentment brings liberty from pride and arrogance. It helps us embrace humility and, therefore, a channel of blessing to others. Contentment will help you remain faithful to God, to your spouse, to your friends and to your family. Embrace contentment. It will help you know how much you need Jesus Christ. This will help you receive and maintain true and lasting blessing. There is no benefit walking in envy. Do everything and pray against envy.

CHAPTER THIRTEEN
The Dangers of Envy

And I saw that all labor and all achievement spring from man's envy of his neighbor.
—ECCLESIASTES 4:4- NIV

THERE ARE DIFFERENT DRIVING FORCES in this world. One of these forces is envy. Envy is the feeling of wishing to have what somebody else has or to be like somebody else. Envy is a taskmaster; it drives people in the wrong direction for very wrong reasons... I have to be like them and have what they have!

Evil Eyes

Evil eyes defy all reason; they are only bent on one thing: the desire to be better than everyone else. It can drive you into premature death. Evil eyes are envious eyes, and eyes of envy will eventually cause us unnecessary stress.

There was a man all alone; he had neither son nor brother.
There was no end to his toil,
yet his eyes were not content with his wealth.
—ECCLESIASTES 4:8

The eyes are never really satisfied. The eyes pry into everything; all they do is lead us into trouble. The above text tells of a young man so driven for wealth that he does not take time to access the direction the desire to be like others is driving him to.

It is important for us to critically assess why the young man above is driven to achieve wealth by ceaseless toil. Why does he not stop or even relax when he is supposed to have more than enough to sustain him? How come he is still dissatisfied, even when he arrives at the point where he has so much that the philosopher is now wondering who he is going to bequeath his excess wealth to?

The answer is simple... He will never get to the point where he can say enough is enough because all this chasing is really a chasing after the wind.

> *"For whom am I toiling," he asked, "and why am I depriving myself of enjoyment?" This too is meaningless- a miserable business!*

Covet Not

Envy drives us into covetousness. A covetous person is one who has or shows a very strong evil desire to possess something that belongs to another. This desire brings its captives into deep bondage. The bondage of covetousness is so deep that it eventually destroys. God hates the covetous with a passion. The last of the Ten Commandments had to do with not coveting anything that belonged to your neighbour.

> *"You shall not covet your neighbor's wife. You shall not set your desire on your neighbor's house or land, his manservant or maidservant, his ox or donkey, or anything that belongs to your neighbor."*
> —DEUTERONOMY 5:21-NIV

A Chasing after the Wind

When men are not content with themselves and with what God has given them, they spend the rest of their lives seeking after what 'other' men seek for. They live their lives virtually to please others. They want what others have, not what they really need. They virtually slave themselves through this life living for others and for things. They have no place for true gratitude in their hearts; they have set their hearts on material things.

All the things you see that others have can never really satisfy you. Chasing after them is engaging in a futile venture. It is even more depressing when you acquire so much, and then you are awakened to the fact that you will depart from this earth penniless.

> *Whoever loves money never has money enough; whoever loves wealth is never satisfied with his income.*
> —ECCLESIASTES 5:10

> *But godliness with contentment is great gain. For, we brought nothing into the world, and we can take nothing out of it.*
> —1TIMOTHY 6:6-7

Be Happy With Your Lot

> *"We often take for granted the very things that most deserve our gratitude."*
> —CYNTHIA OZICK

It is important to realise that true joy and happiness in life is not found in material things. There are couples who have all the money you dream about but are still not happy.

Someone you envy does not have a child. Another person may have children, but the husband has passed. There are some, too, who have money and children, but they are battling all kinds of sicknesses. Where you wished you lived, there are people who live there who wish they did not have so many people of their kind all around them. Some people wish they had less money and more freedom to stay away from all the media attention.

You may admire the young executive who drives the nice, big car. What you do not see is all the stress he has to endure daily that would make your life miserable. Somewhere in a village, a young boy looks high up into the sky and sees a plane. He wishes he would board one, maybe, one day soon. In that same plane, is a pilot who is homesick and is wondering when he can land on the ground again and rest in his own bed.

There is a mother whose son has become a thorn in her flesh because he is on drugs. On the same lane she lives on, is another woman who would do anything to have a son, but the doctors inform her that her fallopian tubes are blocked and her ovaries are bad, and she will have much difficulty having any children of her own.

There is a young, middle-aged man who has started greying and is so worried about the few grey hairs. There is a teenager who would gladly exchange his hairless scalp for few strands of this middle-aged man's hair. Someone is not happy he was born in a poor developing country. Yet there are many born in the so-called developed world that are born blind or have a deformity, and to them, the luxury around them means so little.

There are uneducated, rich businesswomen who have everything many wish and dream about, yet they also envy those who had the privilege of sitting in a classroom. However, some of those who have a good education are not even guaranteed a stable income from a good job. Everybody wishes they were someone else or had what the other person possesses. All fingers are not the same, but all of them are important and have a role to play. Be satisfied with your lot!

Life is all a mirage if you do not have the right perspective. No matter what you have or do not have, life goes on. Your life is certainly better than somebody's somewhere. It begins with first finding inner fulfilment. When that is in place, you will not be bothered about what others have or who they are. Those who have found fulfilment in life have thankful hearts for they know that the Lord is their portion in the land of the living. Grateful people understand that it is good for them to be joyful in life and to find satisfaction with their lot.

> *Then I realized that it is good and proper for a man to eat and drink, and to find satisfaction in his toilsome labor under the sun during the few days of life God has given him, for this is his lot.*
> —ECCLESIASTES 5:18

God bless and keep you.

Other books by the author

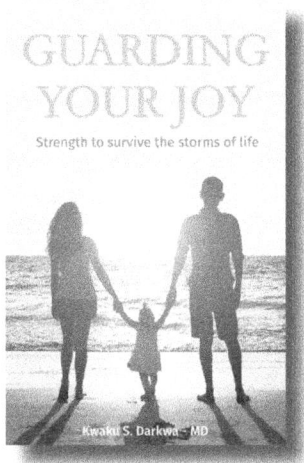

Guarding Your Joy: Strength to Survive the Storms of Life